Clarion Hope

Laurel Luehmann

ISBN: 9798987451601

*For the windblown souls
who have caught the notes of hope's clarion call.
May these words be the hug and the shove that you need.*

contents

prologue   iii

fading scars   1

recovering Eden   23

slaughtered fear   43

many thanks   65

index of poetry by title   67

about the author   69

*Now it is high time to awake out of sleep; for now our salvation
is nearer than when we first believed.
The night is far spent, the day is at hand.
Therefore let us cast off the works of darkness, and let us put
on the armor of light.*

Romans 13:11-12

prologue

crumpled on this tear-stained ground,
I've spent a thousand nights.
a thousand nightmares washed my mind,
a thousand scars now lace my skin.

they're healing now, I see,
as dawn is smothering the darkness.
rays of purple light stretch on this field,
revealing carnage of
a deadly fight.

I hear You stir beside me —
for You guarded all this time —
and the warmth of Your smile now spreads to my soul.
"My daughter, you see? we've won!"

I laugh and embrace You, my heart so full.
in the midst of the battle I made for myself,
You stayed.
You protected.
You loved.

my fingers find Yours and are
welcomed and held.
"Is it time to go home?"
my voice is so weary.

You're shaking Your head now and pulling me close —
my despair melts away into trust.

You hand me the sword of Your spirit
and lean close to whisper to me -

"not quite yet, My darling;
there's so much ahead.
but the battle we fight now…

"I've already won."

fading scars

*come boldly, for His blood has
dissolved all the stains, leaving
scars that bear witness to
grace with no bounds*

unashamed

come into the light;
let your crusted filth fall away.

stand firm
in your shining confidence –
in His robes of righteousness.
let Him burn the old rags,
bringing beauty from ashes.

come into the light,
unashamed.

all

sometimes
the would-have-beens, could-have-beens,
(should-have-beens) won't hold their tongue, and it's
all
too
much.

when the scars are slow to fade,
my fingers trace them
(against my will), and it
all
comes
back…

rushing back with a vengeance,
a wrenching reminder of a girl
(she was me) I once knew
all
too
well -

a girl who leapt before she looked,
wounding those she loved most
(oh, the last thing she wanted) when it
all
fell
apart.

now scars from the fall are the least of her hurt…
the echoes of cries from her victims
(what a word for friends!) are
all
too
much.

I don't want that to be me anymore…
I don't want all these scars
(and those cries) to be
all
they
remember.

oh, God, You see each broken piece -
won't You tell me?
(be honest.) can You heal
all
of
me?

colosseum

once a showcase of
death, depravity, and destruction,
it stands now
broken
yet a symbol of beauty.

if stones once raised by man are such -
Lord, build this from my life!

do you believe Me?

I'm not asking about
My birth as a God-man,
My death as a Savior,
My resurrection as a Victor…

I'm asking about
the sinful thoughts that filled you
last Tuesday,
and the hateful words you spoke
(in your head; I heard them)
last Friday,
and that night from years ago that
still weighs heavy on your heart.

you know I keep no record of those things,
but you keep reminding Me,
again and again and
again.

don't you trust Me when I say
I don't see any of that anymore?
I said I've removed that filth from you
as far as the east is from the west,
so why
are you digging it up again,
rolling in that shame once more?
you're getting the robes I gave you so dirty,
and that's no behavior for
an heir of the King.

lift your head, child, and remember now
Whose you are,
not who you once were.

no stains

stains…
they're all I see
when I look at me.

my past, those sins…
the iron of regret has
seared them on my mind.

I sob and hide my face from You…
heart filled with love, yet
torn by fear and
guilt.

I long to throw the past away
and run to You, but
oh, these stains…

"what stains?"
You ask as You draw me close,
and I catch a glimpse of
nail-scarred hands.

I shake my head and whisper,
"never mind…

"there are no stains."

shattered lies

I lift my eyes
from shattered lies
and raise this pain to You,

knowing You'll make good
what You said You would -
each word You spoke holds true.

and from this death
springs living breath
that longs for souls made new…

I lift my eyes
from shattered lies
and raise this pain to You.

dare to hope

rest, My love…
rise up from the shards of these broken dreams
and let your heart soar again.

dare to dream that there's more than
this broken road
and that beauty may lie
on tomorrow's edge.

hope, My love.
dare to hope.

furnaces

with You, I can see beyond this desert -
on Your shoulders,
I see hope dancing on the horizon,
the truth that
there is more than this suffering…
and this pain will turn to gold
in the furnaces of time.

buried hopes

You see these dreams I've lodged
deep in this soil -
the loves I've forgotten
For the sake of Your own.

'tis better, I know,
to delight in Your ways
than to cling to the dreams
You have asked me to leave…

it aches, Lord, to feel
such a pull toward dead hopes
I once treasured - oh, help me
march on with no tears!

shreds

I threw that away…

but here you are
every day
chasing me down with that
shred of my past
that I left in the dust
now I shake it from your hands
again
leave it on the sand
for the waves to wash away, yeah

I'm done with you today.

renouncement

etch the tale in silver: how
we'll break the chains of the past asunder,
and kindle a fire of
paper-thin ghosts
that once proudly bore our faces…

(for that's you and me no longer.)

safely home

some days
I see so clearly.
the road ahead is winding,
but I face the next bend with
courage and excitement,
joy lighting my eyes and
quickening my step.

other days
I trip on fallen limbs from the past.
bruised and bleeding,
old scars torn again,
I long to curl up -
a defeated mess of sweat and tears -
in the middle of this road.
it would be far easier
to be the girl I once was…
hopeless.
tearful.
broken.

but You walk beside me,
strengthening me for
one more step,
one more smile,
one more fight.

thus lead me, Love,
until I'm safely home.

happy ending

bathed in His light,
all the scars turned to tales
of His faithfulness shining
against all the odds.

greater things

You call me onwards…
out of these ashes and
into Your dreams, where
You'll do even greater things
than these.

no regrets

no regrets -
they say that's foolishness
when they see all my scars
and the mess I've left behind.

they see the ashes, but
I see the beauty…

for I trust that each shard is a
sword for tomorrow
in my Father's hand.

glimmer

see, even teardrops
glimmer in the face of light,
defying darkness

broken record

an irreversible crack
spiderwebs across
the mirror of the past, and
all I see
in its image of the future is
the portrait of endless depravity…
a broken record that
croaks a trashy song
over and over and over
until my voyages around the sun are
complete.

I gaze into the face of
the Truth-Speaker,
and reflected in His eyes I see
a chance to break the brokenness -
and the hammer lies in
His nail-scarred hand.

hope's clarion call

turn from the west -
a flaming horizon where heartache and fear
have now met their match.
those plains - scarred with battle -
must be left behind, for the east
and new radiance are calling…

look now!
turn your eyes to the east
and see life dawning bright,
hope's clarion call ringing sweet in your ears.
walk away from what's passed -
we move on to the hills -
to fight towards the light and its Master -

come now!
we turn from what's passed and
fight on.

recovering Eden

a deluded world
applauds
the ghosts unshaken by its filth.

all hail the strength of
the tender heart
that ceases not to
weep at sin.

shalom

a broken world is gasping
for the wholeness of shalom.

"peace!" they cry -
there is no peace…
it's all a lovely lie.

"peace," they plead,
and shove a crown of thorns
upon its Prince's head.

"peace," they weep,
and grasp at shreds of
calm -

they miss shalom.

maranatha

do you ever fear that
the beauty of those days -
so sweet
so innocent
so unbelievably right -
may never come again?

because I do.

I stand here, staring at
brokenness, and
I weep.
I weep because all of this used to be
so sweet
so innocent
so unbelievably right…
but now?
it's ugly.
not even ugly…

it's commonplace, and that's what I fear.
I fear the current of the commonplace.
I ache for the thrill of
unthrottled beauty
sweetness
innocence…
righteousness.
each piece of my soul aches for all of this to be
right.

for all of the broken farewells —
the goodbyes that weren't good —
to be made right.
for all of the loneliness to be
washed away in the
waters of unity.
for all of the hatred to
dissolve in forgiveness.
for all of this —
all of us —
to be healed.

oh, my soul screams,
maranatha!

like Mine

I still wore pigtails when
I ran to You, sobbing,
fists full of the shards I'd found of a
sin-shattered world.
the brokenness broke me, and
even as You wept
and comforted
and held me close,
I saw joy glinting deep in Your eyes.
"her heart…
it beats like Mine."

years passed

so many shards sliced my heart
again and again

and I run to You now,
shards still clenched in my palms,
still sobbing
and sobbing
and sobbing…

You cup my teary face in
hands gentle in their power,
and in the eyes that gaze into mine,
I still see joy mixed with the pain.

"let them go," You whisper, and
one by one
I watch each sanguine piece fall
at Your feet.

in Your embrace
I feel tears in my hair, and
the rhythm of Your breaking heart
beats a symphony of joy.

vandalism

they've taken the temples You built
with such care,
and filled them with thoughts
so repulsive to you.
notions dripping with sin and
steeped in the stench of their pride are
paraded before
the holiest place.

iniquity pools on the unswept floors, and
scavenging lust laps it ravenously,
never full.

in a brash, careless hand,
"I know better" is scrawled
in the dust that has gathered
on top of the altar.

oh, El Roi, how long?
how long?

glutted

You've called us to more
than this man-made feast
of base cravings and lust and deceit –
but we gorge
our flabby hearts on it, and
ask why it stings
to look at our souls in Your mirror and
see
we're not who we're meant to be.

there's more…
so much more…

have we courage to step from this table?

monuments

we build our little kingdoms,
bolstering our fragile mortality with
towers that reach for the sky,
monuments screaming our names, and
words on paper that will only outlast us for decades.

for the winds of change must blow,
eroding the days of our pilgrimage from
tombstones that sink in the loam,
washing the proof of our self-importance into
the dust from whence we came.

even now

You're near to me,
and I can't see
why he won't draw near to You.

my heart still breaks with
each step she takes
away from what is true.

but I know that You're the Shepherd
who will leave the ninety-nine
and Your promises will never fail -
You're faithful every time.

so I wait here in the darkness,
the horizon glowing now,
and each prayer is breathed in trust -
my Love, You're faithful
even now.

shadowed

the harsh shadows of
a superficial world and
its superficial shadows
(though they masquerade as men)
are far too small -
their tower of Babel leaves me
underwhelmed and groping for
much more.

I close my eyes and I can see
a world where colors dance
and laughter is not shallow.
a place where "how are you today?"'s
are met with truth, and
"wonderful!" is truth.

the light of that world swirls deep in my soul,
and I fling it out like ribbons
on the shadows that surround me.

someday the life that shines in my mind
will be the world I see.

last night

the woods were alive last night…
fingers of poplars stretched at the edge
for the sky as they guarded
a gilded carpet of orange.
through the maples and oaks,
a rock face stared boldly,
daring the world to
step from the beaten path and
behold its majesty.
but I couldn't.
the day was slipping away, and
the field wouldn't tend itself.

I cried alone in the field last night…
for all the souls I'll never know,
all the sunsets I'll never see,
all the love I've failed to give,
all the chances I've lost and will lose…
but Yahweh reigns outside of time,
and soon this clock-bound shell will fall
for good, and last nights
(and their tears)
will all be
gone.

rumblings

I let go
any rights I think I have to
resolution.

weeping,
I lay broken, untold stories
in Your hands,
Your promises of better tales
held close against
my racing heart.

I listen,
my ear pressed against
this shattered earth,
rumblings of hope
pulsing strong deep below.
I smile to know
there is more than meets the eye.

the in-between

I will praise You here
with unclenched hands
in the middle of an empty field
while barren branches sing
in the wind that
stripped them of their glory.

perhaps
You've taken
(as You did with the trees)
each lovely bit I didn't need
in a masterful plan to
clothe my soul in
the glory of the next season.

even so, my Love…
even so…

Lord, be my cloak and comfort
in the ache of the in-between.

roaming love

they say that grief is simply love…
a roaming love that finds
no resting place.

a love forbidden from release…
a love that must be bottled,
stored until
eternity.

grandpa

I never saw it coming,
your leaving.
you were invincible -
scarred, yet invincible -
and I never doubted it until
lights flashed in the yard
longer than you could
put it on reserve.
I knew.

I knew you were gone before
I saw each fighting, dying gasp.

I wished that Friday evening back,
when your smile could answer my voice…
but God called it enough,
and I rest in His plan, somehow,
through the "what if"s…
giving each goodbye hug with
more thought and
awaiting the day when
days melt into glory.

to dance again

if I seem callous as you weep with the weight of their
grief,
if my tearless "I'm sorry"s seem careless and cruel,
please, *(please)*
know that I'm not.
oh, I'm not…
far behind my stiff upper lip
I'm crying inside,
still fighting to heal the bruises
left by the fists of a dying world.

I don't ignore their pain.
for now I can only take it in shaking fingers,
tucking it away in the corner of my heart where
I bottle the pain for the moments

when I can be alone…
in my car or
the pastures or
the bedroom I haven't tidied yet today…
alone with the pain
(all the pain)
and the silence and
the God who heals broken things.

I uncork the pain and
pour it all out before Him -
all of it, with the tears and the ache that comes, too,
for
it's far, far too much for
this mortal's heart.

here they are, Father…

the "I love you"s that were twisted,
not what love was meant to mean…

the knowledge that a kindred spirit is sleeping alone
on a tear-dewed pillow in the moonlight tonight…
(oh, God!)

and that song I'll never finish,
and the letters I'll never send…

the words I should have said and
the words I never should have…
(oh, Father!)

the souls with broken minds
who will never again know innocence…

all of it threatens to make me
a stoop-souled girl behind
this ready smile.

it's much too much for this heart to bear…

so I hand it to the Healer
in tears
and find I can dance again.

recovering Eden

I can scarcely believe
who I am in Your arms.
in Your healing hands, my fearful soul rose
safe in Your holiness,
emboldened by Your love to
obtain promises,
subdue kingdoms,
and stop the mouths of lions.
You make me valiant in battle,
and the me of last year would scarcely recognize
the warrior in the mirror:
windblown hair crowned with roses,
my eyes full of wonder,
healed heart beating hard for
my King and His kingdom.

I pick up my sword -
a rose falls from my hair,
a gentle reminder that
beauty, redemption, recovering Eden
are the whys behind my war.

rose close to my heart and
sword clenched in my fist,
I walk towards the light,
to heal or to fight,
my ear tuned to the voice of my King.

slaughtered fear

if I fear not death…
if the Defender holds my future…
if fear does not control me…

then what, pray, can steal my courage?

tread these paths

observe, My child,
the ways that I walk,
and tread these paths beside Me.

the world dances to a different tune,
so press your ear close to My song and
obey
these words that I sing to you,
lest you forget in the valley
the songs that we sang on the mountaintop,
for My words still ring true in the storm.
take My hand, little one,
for I long to be near you,
and shield you from fear
and the terror of night.

observe, My child,
the ways that I walk,
and tread these paths beside Me.

tales of courage

I thought tales of courage were
traced in blood on foreign shores…
and so I prayed that I might be given a ticket to glory
via lands I'd never seen.

I grew up
and watched childhood friends fly away
to wage the Spirit's war in
cities whose names my tongue couldn't grasp
while my feet stayed rooted,
a ridgetop girl…

and I began to read tales of courage
traced in the smile lines of
the minutes-old widow spinning fanciful tales
from the straws of grief that sought to overwhelm.

I saw them shining in the eyes of the woman
who rejoiced at the birth of new lives
while her own aching arms hung empty.

I saw them in the limping stride of the farmer
who refused to forsake his land or stock
in the years that stretched on with no profit.

and I saw a horizon stretch before me -
a beckoning to this same quiet courage
that lives and dies unnoticed.

so I'll trace tales of courage on windblown ridgetops
where few feet will ever walk,
trusting the increase to the One who called…

oh, El Roi, this is enough.

enough

only one voice in thousands,
drowned by a wave of iniquity.

if the world does not hear my voice,
still the Just One does,
and, quiet though it is
in the ears of the world,
it is raised with a passion
for light to prevail…

and He calls that enough.

when You veil the way

walking by faith
in the midst of the storm
in the dark of the night
when the veil isn't torn
when the answers You give
aren't revealed to me yet,
still I'll trust

(trust Him, my soul)

songs in the night
are the comfort You give
and the peace You hold out
every day that I live
is the strength of my heart
when my courage has died…
still I'll trust

(trust Him, my soul)

untrodden

when You called to me gently
and held out Your hand with such longing and love,
I vowed I would follow You
anywhere.

but really, God?
here?

we're off the beaten path,
and everyone's giving me dubious looks
as dust stirs around their faithful feet
in the well-worn path of convention
while I'm headed straight for
the wild tangle of the forest.

it's lonely here.
a bit painful, too.

But I look up from my weary feet
(one foot in front of the other; keep going)
and You're still here beside me, smiling.
"I'm taking you where no one's been before.
you'll claim new territory.
win fearsome battles.
touch broken hearts.
live a life for which
those too fearful to leave the path
can only long."

somehow the pack on my back lightens
as His words make it a privilege.

the chisel

why do I despise
these waiting hands?
empty
trembling
expectant…

why do I fear
what You'll give me next? for
I've seen the way You work.

I've seen You turn
ashes to beauty
scars into art
so why am I afraid that
Your chisel will slip this time?

oh, Father, steel my trembling soul…
make it unflinching beneath the blade.

the squall

the storm is raging, and I can't see how
You'll make a way
through these troubled waves.
I know Your heart, and
I know Your might,
but it's hard to trust
in the midst of this squall.
I know You work where I can't see,
I know You're so much wiser,
but I feel afraid -
Lord, hold me close
in the middle of this storm.

wardrobe

I'm Lucy in the wardrobe,
Bilbo at his door,
Mary at the garden's edge,
Jo longing for New York…

afraid to leave behind the world
and life I've always known,
afraid to lead a different life
than what this land has known…

but what songs will not be sung,
and what tales will not be told
if I venture not outside my door
to burgle dragons' gold?

unhindered grace

turn my eyes
from all that threatens
to distract and destroy
the intimacy of this moment with You.
let outside problems melt away
as my soul curls into Yours
unhindered
by fears I'm not born to have.

may I see You clearly
with longing eyes
that see beyond this storm,
and glimpse a bit of eternity
as I gaze into Your face.

oh, give me Your eyes
to see each battle as already fought and won,
to see the gasping souls behind each cruel shell…
to see the strength infused
by You
into this timid, clumsy soul
in these moments of unhindered grace
as I gaze into Your face.

I can be brave

I can be brave.

not because I am strong, for
this torn, battered will
lies here shattered by
fear and the "what ifs" that
swarm in my mind, no

I can be brave, for
He tells me I've won.

freefall

life's an adventure -
I won't miss a beat.
let me stand on the edge of my fears and
freefall,
not wasting a breath in my lungs.

let me soar
above trivialities, groping for more
of Your beauty and grace
until I see Your face and gasp,
"Jesus, I gave it my all."

spirit

and if fear roars, my love…
you shove it down with
this bit of truth:
the Spirit within you, it
laughs in the face of fear.
it's swollen with power,
fierce in love,
and clothed with the strength of
an anchored mind.

oh, struggle assured…
we *will* overcome.

barricades

the solid walls you built
so many years ago
are here for the moments such as these
when passion pleads persistently
and leaves you breathless
incapable
of stemming its flood.

let them stand the test of time
and young infatuation, for

'tis better to ache for a moment than to
weep over rubble.

not today

not today, Satan…
your feet have trampled enough
well-meaning souls.
your hands have throttled
more warriors than I can count.
your schemes have knocked too many
kingdom-builders flat on their backs.

so I'm taking a stand -
one hand holding high the shield of faith,
the other the sword of the Spirit you hate.
see, I'm not the girl you knew way back when…
my ear is too close to the song of the King
to heed traitors.

I'm sorry, not sorry -
you can't crush the Bride
of the One who crushed your head.

brave

the word's been
cheapened, weakened,
twisted, glazed…

now no one wants
the real, raw thing
in worn work boots that
trudges on,
steeling the hearts of the faithful.

perhaps

perhaps courage isn't so much
chasing your dreams with no fear
as it is
laying them down with no fear.

perhaps it is more
learning to die to the world than
learning to earn the praise of the world.

it may be that
courage yields where cowards fight.

perhaps the most courageous thing to do is
to seem a fool
in the bloodshot eyes of the world.

Now may the God of hope
fill you with all joy and peace in believing,
that you may abound in hope
by the power of the Holy Spirit.

Romans 15:13

many thanks

"I couldn't have done it without you" is cliché because it's so true. Even the wild "I'll do it myself or die trying" indie authors (such as myself) would never make it anywhere without the kindred spirits who prop them up along the way.

My family – I can't thank you enough for listening patiently when I feel the need to ramble, for believing in me when I can't, and for filling my life with laughter (even if it is at me) and good conversations. I love waging war beside you on our ridgetop battlefields.

Mommy – for listening to me cry through the first draft of this book, for the texts of encouragement, and for everything I'll never think to thank you for giving. I love you so much.

Abby – for your honesty and constant willingness to read whatever I shove in front of you, and for the late-night talks about all things ridiculous and earth shaking. Thank you for being such a gracious Woodstock. ♥ Snoopy

Grandma – thank you for being my fellow poet, role model, and dear friend all rolled into one…I love our sleepovers and British movie nights. (Let's have another one soon.)

Alexandria – words don't go far enough. Your warrior's heart and nurturing spirit have changed me in ways I can't express. Thank you for always being there to prop up my soul with Scripture and quotable lines (in spite of miles and time zones), for reading and giving feedback so willingly, and for the meaning of blue roses. Here's to many more years of sharing potatoes and poetry!

Kristina – for the deep talks, the dark chocolate peanut butter cups, and all of the encouragement and time you've given. You are an answer to prayer, my friend.

Victoria – so much of the fiery nature of this book has been stoked by your soul. Thank you for speaking the truth with boldness and love, and for so kindly helping me over the technical bumps in the road. You have no idea how much of a blessing you are.

Those who have cheered me on as I continue scribbling – thank you for the enthusiasm, the writing prompts, and the potato memes. Truly your encouragement has been a heaven-sent blessing!

Jim and Elisabeth Elliot. Amy Carmichael. Oswald Chambers. Peter/Cephas. William Wilberforce. Gladys Aylward – only the first that come to mind of many who have impacted my mind and life solely through the legacy they left. Thank you for planting seeds of courage in the mind of a timid little girl just by living your lives with boldness for the glory of our Savior. I can't wait to meet you all.

El Roi…words could never go far enough, and yet you ask me to come boldly. Thank You for leading me gently through each step of this process and tying together all of the loose ends I never noticed. I am forever in awe of You. You have never despised a single *Jesu, juva*, and it's only by that grace I can cry out

SOLI DEO GLORIA.

index of poetry by title

title	page number
all	4
barricades	58
brave	60
broken record	21
buried hopes	13
chisel, the	51
colosseum	6
dare to hope	11
do you believe Me?	7
enough	48
even now	33
freefall	56
furnaces	12
glimmer	20
glutted	31
grandpa	39
happy ending	17
hope's clarion call	22
I can be brave	55
in-between, the	37
last night	35
like Mine	28
maranatha	26
monuments	32
no regrets	19
no stains	9
not today	59
perhaps	61
recovering Eden	42
renouncement	15

rumblings 36
roaming love 38
safely home 16
shadowed 34
shalom 25
shattered lies 10
shreds 14
spirit 57
squall, the 52
tales of courage 46
to dance again 40
tread these paths 45
unashamed 3
unhindered grace 54
untrodden 50
vandalism 30
wardrobe 53
when You veil the way 49

about the author

Laurel Luehmann has a passion for capturing the raw beauty and emotion of life in words to share with the world. Some of her happiest moments are spent chatting with kindred spirits, mashing potatoes, singing and playing the guitar with gusto, and dairy farming with her family in the Midwest.

Website: laurel-luehmann.com
Instagram: @laurel_luehmann_writer

www.ingramcontent.com/pod-product-compliance
Lightning Source LLC
Chambersburg PA
CBHW022054150726
47990CB00003B/1079